GREECE

TIGER BOOKS INTERNATIONAL

Text
Simonetta Crescimbene

Graphic design
Patrizia Balocco

Contents

2-3 Situated on top of the Acropolis, the calcareous upland overlooking the Attic plain and the capital city, the fortified "high town" boasts monuments dating back to the Classical Age.

4-5 This picture shows in detail the western façade of the Parthenon, richly decorated with sculptured reliefs.

6-7 The twenty monasteries and the numerous tiny hermitages clinging to the rocks of Mount Athos have a total population of 1,500. This photograph shows the Great Lavra Monastery.

8 The tiny island of Santorini, or Thera, in the Cyclades, has some 365 churches.

9 Mykonos, in the Cyclades, boasts a traditional tourist attraction in the windmills that line its coast; each year the windmills are repainted a blinding white.

10-11 The white terraces slope down to the sea on Santorini, also known as Thera.

12-13 The remains of a ship washed ashore on Zante, an Ionian island.

14-15 Only fifteen Doric columns still remain from Poseidon's Temple, built at Cape Savio in the fifth century B.C. Visitors' names, including Lord Byron's, are engraved on one of the columns.

This edition published in 1994 by TIGER BOOKS INTERNATIONAL PLC , 26a York Street Twickenham TW1 3LJ, England.

First published by Edizioni White Star. Title of the original edition: Grecia, sulla rotta di Odisseo. © World copyright 1993 by Edizioni White Star. Via Candido Sassone 22/24, 13100 Vercelli, Italy.

ISBN 1-85501-293-6

Printed in Singapore by Tien Wah Press Color separations by Magenta, Lit. Con., Singapore.

Introduction

Sophocles asserted: "There are so many wonders in the world, but none of them is more wonderful than man," and Socrates, looking at the extraordinary Attic landscape, affirmed in his *Phaedra*: "Landscapes and trees could not teach me anything; only the inhabitants of the city could do it." No other civilization was as proud of man himself as the Greek one. The Greeks carved marble into lifelike depictions of the human body, in search of a perfect balance; they explored the human spirit in subtle philosophical endeavor. Greece was the cradle of poetry.

The variegated, folkloristic landscape tourists enter today can hardly be separated from its inhabitants' personality — the same as that described in the wise words of their poets. The desolate beaches where Odysseus, exhausted after the shipwreck of his raft, was discovered by Nausicaä, and where Achilles, offended by Agamemnon, retired to talk to the waves, still maintain the tragic quality that makes them unique.

Today, the industry and dedication of the Greek people is tangible in the tiny rural villages, in the winding paths through the mountains, where oil lamps burn in chapels dedicated to the patron saint of these heights, and even on the open sea, in "the moonlight which turns white the land," as Sappho described it. Perhaps the secret of the country's Mediterranean charm is revealed through these images, ancient and contemporary at the same time, which induce thousands of tourists to set out each year to discover the Greek Islands. Travel in this land in a voyage through a broadening panorama of time and a journey into one's own soul: the final destination is knowledge, remembering, and harmony - a rediscovery of life. Mnemosyne, the muse of memory for the ancients,

is often a tutelary deity, leading the modern, nostalgic pilgrimages of people who studied Greek poets in school.

This country is endowed with a profundity of culture that is not betrayed even by the giddiest merrymaking; in this cradle of Western civilization, hilarity has always been considered a form of freedom, a liberation of the spirit. The Latins adopted this point of view and often subscribed to the famous saying: *Semel in anno licet insanire* — "Once a year you are allowed to act like a fool." In Italy during the Middle Ages, the feast of fools freed people from the strictness of Christian dogma. Dionysus, god of wine and ecstasy, is the ancient master of all intemperances. Alcaeus and other poets wrote in favor of the worship of Dionysus, pointing out therapeutic effects: "Heroic medicine is plenty of wine and inebriety," and, "Where there is wine, there is a real man." Plentiful wine, the sweet Mavrodafne, for example, is served in the old quarters in Athens by waiters with names such as Pericles and Themistocles.

A symbol of this ebullient spirit is Kazantzakis's indomitable Zorba the Greek, whom he described in this way: "He seemed to be made of rubber; clapping his hands, jumping up and down, falling on his bended knees, he defied the forces of gravity as if he wanted to break the laws of nature by flying in the air." In nearby Skyros, once a year the bold young men dress up as anthropomorphic billy goats and upset the daily rhythm of life with an impudent ritual which is in no way inferior, in passion or presence, to the wild dances of the Bac-chantes, in their animal hides, as tradition of the ancient Hellas. In Hellenistic times, no aspect of life, frivolous or serious, could be ignored. An enlightening metaphor is handed down, attributed to Pythagoras. It compares human life with the feasts at Olympia, where some came on business, some came to take part in the races, some came to enjoy themselves, and the philosophers came to observe it all.

Our ancestors were scrupulous chroniclers of their time. Pausanias, with his subtle observations, describes a route through the ruins of the ancient splendors and their heritage. The *Description of Greece*, an old guidebook, introduces the sanctuary at Olympia in this way: "Many things are

16 *This bronze statue of a young man from Antikythera, dating from 340 B.C., by an unknown sculptor, is at the National Archaeological Museum in Athens.*

17 top *Bronze casting was used to mold the noble features of this charioteer from Delphi; to add incisiveness to his expression, the artist used enamel. The statue stands 6 feet tall, and dates from the late archaic period.*

17 bottom *The National Archaeological Museum devotes a great deal of space to the findings of Heinrich Schliemann in Mycenae. The famous gold mask, ascribed to Agamemnon by some, is among them.*

18-19 *Gournia is the only urban settlement of the Minoan civilization to be discovered along the northern coast of Crete. Paved lanes separate the ruins of houses and workshops dating back to the 16th century B.C.*

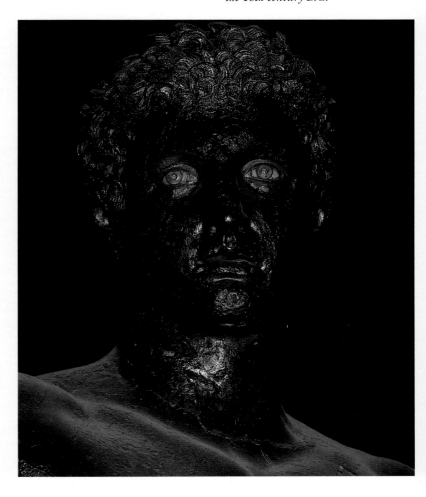

to be seen in Greece, and many others to be heard, but nothing is more divine than the Eleusinian mysteries and the Olympic contests."

At the foot of the Kronion, or Hill of Cronus, at the confluence of two rivers, the Alpheus and the Cladeus, stands Altis, the sacred grove consecrated to Zeus. Green and rich in trees and plants, it holds numerous monuments and was the setting for heroic legends and clever political and military enterprises. Here, propitiatory rites and sacrifices and exciting contests took place, and we have received a collection of anecdotes about both the vanquished and the victors. Pagan gods, according to the legend were the first to meet in this place.

In 776 B.C. the stadium of Olympia was the site of the first Olympic contests. They were first limited to 180-meter races, and then numerous different contests were added. The *diaulos* was the double round race, the *dolichos* a long-distance race. Then came the pentathlon, the *pankration*, boxing, cart races, and horse races. Even young boys competed in these contests.

Altis soon became a lively center for the celebration of athletics, while the imposing temple of Zeus rose up with its 39 feet-high statue of the god. Phidias, the famous Athenian sculptor, designed this monument in a large workshop on the edge of the sacred soil. Pausanias is rapt as he describes this now-lost wonder in detail; he speaks of how the throne, enlivened with a sculptured frenzy of dancing goddesses and Theban maidens — all carved in ivory and ebony — was adorned with gold and precious stones. Was it destroyed to comply with Emperor Theodosius's aversion to pagan monuments, or was it swallowed by the Cladeus's waters? Perhaps some day the temple that influenced the old world so much will be given back by the river, considered by the ancients to be an irritable god, but by the more sensible people of today to be nothing more than a stream.

This harmonious gymnasium changed in appearance not only because of the quarrels and the envies of the pagan gods but also as a result of the ravages of time. Ornaments and brightly colored tympanums and colonnades that stood out clearly against the blue sky were wiped out, and today only a vast panorama can be admired. Modern tourists can wander through the traces of high columns or the ruins of a peristyle, and from the inscriptions, identify the gymnasium and the stadium.

When these ruins stood solid, every dispute between opposing factions was suspended when the Olympic games were in progress. In this way, the principles of peace, often denied by military politics, were reaffirmed, along with the sacredness of the contest, which reached its peak when the winners crossed the finish line near the temple of Zeus, where they were received by Nike, the goddess of victory. The Greeks, flaunting their riches and prestige in the votive temples built by the city-states, were the forerunners of the modern sponsors so fashionable today.

Situated in Delphi is the *temenos*, the holy enclosure said to hold nothing less than the center of the world. The legend tells us that Zeus, father of all gods, set two eagles free from the two opposite limits of the globe. They met in flight over Delphi, and a stone, the *omphalos*, was placed there to mark the navel of earth. Such legends ensured spiritual supremacy and fame for this site, first consecrated to Gaea, goddess of earth, and then to Apollo, god of light. Visitors who travel along the Holy Way today — the same route of pilgrimages dating back some 2,500 years and climbing up the slope of Mount Parnassus — are destined to revere nature.

The Phaedriades, (called "the shining" because they turned fiery red at sunset) were two rocky headlands that met in a gorge where the Castalian Spring gushed forth. It was here that the ritual of purification took place for those who wanted to consult the most famous oracle of ancient times. Canny priests put the obscure responses into verse. They could concern any subject, including religion and business, marriage, and, by popular demand, the ideal locations for colonies. The Pythia delivered the oracles; at times the press of consultants was so great that there were two Pythias on duty and one in reserve. In periods of great popularity, Phytia, seated on the sacred throne in the underground cell of the temple, multiplied herself three times in order to make history through predictions. Whether the mephitic fumes came from a split in the rock or from some other source, these "visions" met with very ambiguous results. Croesus, king of Lydia,

learned this at his peril: when he asked for a prediction about a hypothetical attack against the Persians, the cryptic vestal answered that he would destroy a large empire, but did not explain that the empire he destroyed would be his own. The dangerous misunderstandings to which the "customers" of the sanctuary fell prey did nothing to damage the oracle's reputation, and generous gifts were showered upon Delphi, many of them now the pride and joy of important museums around the world.

And now we come to some unique "museums." Their uniqueness is due to the fact that they are inhabited. They are the monasteries of Mount Athos, declared a republic under Greek protection in the early twentieth century. Mount Athos is a holy promontory located on the peninsula of Chalcidic, where inner secrets of Byzantine art are preserved. The appearance of this holy region leads us to think it was intended for more-than-earthly inhabitants; the hills climb steadily upward the towering Mount Athos. Along the mountainside, monasteries and hermitages are set on the impervious rock as if they were the nests of ancient winged creatures. These places, devoted to the orthodox faith, overlook the sea - and water so clear that it seems to have been filtered. The practice of asceticism is necessary for those who, having been granted *diamonitirion*, or permission, cross the secular thresholds seeking the monastic life. The Esphygmenou monastery, whose tower bears a flag with the gloomy inscription "Orthodoxy or death," is situated overlooking a bay. This microcosm, this theocratic republic, is like a tightrope strung through an extremist spirit that compensates for the absolute uprightness, asceticism and idiorrhythmic aspect (*idios*, personal; *rhythmos*, rhythm) of the life.

The ethnic derivation is largely Greek, although there is a Bulgarian group at Zagraphou, a Yugoslavian group at Chilandari, and a Russian group at Panteleimon. These monks are, today, elderly and few in number, because the political situation in Russia has caused the religious vocation to dwindle in recent decades. Under the Greek sky, the view of the variegated flags wrapping around the domes brings a peaceful feeling, and inside every monastery the *Katholikon*, the sanctuary shared by all religious people, rises toward a celestial dome filled with representations of saints surrounding the Almighty. A fantastic array of color rises from these high domes evoking the evangelical texts. During the religious functions, the fusion of these flags of shot silk evokes an image of faith and beauty.

Some 1,500 monks devote themselves to sustaining, through work and prayer, twenty monasteries, a few small villages, and, along the southern coast, tiny, frail hermitages built on sheer cliffs above the sea. In these inaccessible hermitages, the contemplations of the monks are disturbed only when supplies are lowered by pulley in order to feed them to ensure their good health. The hermits were the first to settle in the peninsula. Little by little, it conformed to the ideal of a spiritual colony surviving according to rules of frugality and industry that St. Athanasius preached in 963. Unfortunately, the rules of the saint have prohibited, through the centuries, the presence of women.

In Thessaly, the monasteries of A´ia Triás, the Great Meteoron and Varlaám, and Roussanou are kept by monks whose features are deeply marked by the ravages of time, and their way of thinking defies with firm determination the Heraclitean principle *Panta rhei*, "Everything changes." They are the descendants of the great Byzantine artists, and, in cells that have been turned into workshops, they craft iconographies according to the dictates of thousand-year-old traditions. These men are the keepers of exclusive secrets, handed down in the oral tradition like codes containing ancestral wisdom.

The surreal landscape from which the marvelous "monasteries in the air" emerge boasts stone towers that inspire amazement. The tourists wait for the lowering of the net that at the beginning of the century raised the novices to the top of the huge spur. This spell is occasionally broken when groups of tourists go bumping by on mountain bikes along the winding downhill paths, or when people fond of free climbing try to conquer, inch by inch, the natural harshness of the rock.

Wisdom and spirituality are virtues ascribed to

20 *The Olympic stadium, built near Athens in recent years, is full of life during the opening of the European Championship of Athletics.*

21 *Greek athletes parade along the Olympic circuit, waving the white and blue symbol of their mother country.*

the Greek world; they became important when the first metaphysicians, under the plane trees, meditated and instructed others on the existence of the *arché* or fundamental life force. According to some, water was the vital source from which everything began, while others ascribed the same importance to fire and air. Anaximander established the concept of *apeiron*, the unlimited. It would have been naive to predict a different evolution of thought in the country of the "Milesian wise man," who, in 600 B.C., attributed a soul to even a magnet, because it attracted iron. In this way, he reaffirmed his belief that "Everything is full of God."

In recent times, strong religious feeling has been the cohesive element that has favored the uniting of the territory divided by the mountains and subdivided into more than 2,000 islands. On May 21 of each year, Agia Eleni, Agios Petros, and Laganda celebrate the *Anastenaria*, dancing together on burning lumps of coal with icons in their hands. In mid-August, the Cult of the Virgin is so strong a presence in the areas from the Ionian to the Mediterranean and from here to the Aegean Sea that hymns are sung seemingly in unison. History has provided these places with saints, blessed souls, and martyrs, all of whom have found a place on the calendar. In this way, one has the opportunity to celebrate almost daily festivities. Everyone and every place has a saint to turn to: the sailors to St. Nicholas, artillerymen and firemen to St. Barbara, Athens to St. Denis.

The most moving holiday, consistent with the identity of these people, is Easter. In the evening on Good Friday, the believers with their candles walk in procession to the "Sepulchre" which is covered with violets and lilacs. On the island of Karpathos, it is the custom to make the *epitaphios* — a cross, decorated with thousands of flowers, upon which the photos of family members who died during the year are placed; situated in front of the church, it attracts attention on Friday night when the Passion of Christ is at the peak of its pathos. Women give themselves up to growing moans, which turn to tears and even screams, in a painful, unrestrained ecstasy; they undo their braids and plaited hair with desperate gestures.

The resurrection of Christ is celebrated on

Saturday, when the clock strikes midnight in all church courtyards in the cities and the country. When only the echo of the Pope's psalms can be heard, the people break their fast; in the privacy of their own homes, they have traditional tripe soup. *Christos Anesti*, "Christ is risen," *Alithos Anesti*, "He is really risen" — this unchanging dialogue is acted out by the citizens as a ritual, while colorful Easter eggs are placed in the middle of the traditional ring-shaped cakes.

On the Feast of the Ascension, in the clear spring air fragrant with flowers, Christ's ascent to heaven is celebrated, with dancing around the spit which bears the sacrificial lamb. Female mourners replace their dark and austere clothes with multicolored traditional costumes of shiny silk and necklaces of gold coins. They are caught up in the whirl of the *tsamikos* and the *kalamatianos* (similar to the farandola, a Provençal dance), by the sound of the clarion and *santouri* (a harplike instrument), and by the lyre.

This country, whose inhabitants display both a deep-rooted passion and a sober wisdom, promises to evoke strong emotions in travelers from all over the world.

Moving on, we come to the territory of the Muses, inspirers of poetry. They are neither on Mount Parnassus with their sisters, the patrons of the arts, as the Latin legend tells us, nor on Olympus, where they danced with the Graces at the feasts of the gods, but in Arcadia, the plateau in the middle of Peloponnesus, unchanged, over millennia. Since the dawning of this civilization, poets have affirmed, as Archilochus did, "I am the master of the Muse's feverish gift," perceiving themselves as conduits for Calliope, Erato, Melpomene, Thalia, and Polyhymnia.

The Olympus that was once so difficult to reach and which excluded mortals from its feverish orgies, with resinous wine and ambrosia, is now a renowned ski resort. Everywhere, hills are covered by silver olive trees, twisted descendants of more illustrious ones, looked after in the nursery of the gods (Altis) for the production of the *Kotinos*, or olive garland, which was used to crown the tenacious winners in Olympia. The splendid light which once followed the awakening of nymphs and fauns makes this country an economical center rich

22 *The Corinth Canal was built between 1881 and 1893. nine yards deep, 3.9 miles long, and 25 yards wide, it allows the passage of ships up to 10,000 tons.*

23 *The port of Piraeus was built by Themistocles after 482 B.C., and since then it has been the most important Greek port of call. The principal structure, Cantharus, is flanked by two ancient, secondary ports. Others are under construction in order to lighten the traffic.*

24-25 *The Island of Kastellorizon of today was known as Megiste. It is the easternmost Greek island; it faces the coast of Turkey.*

25 *Sunset lights up the village on Khalki Island, near Rhodes.*

in cultivation and cattle farms. The delicious fruits of Argos, the olives of Kalamata, and the unique grapes of Corinth, arranged in never-ending rows until they reach the capital, adorn with variety and Mediterranean flavor the tables of the *moreano*, the inhabitant of the Peloponnesus, and the *rumeliota*, the inhabitant of continental Greece.

Thousands of varied attractions capture the attention of the visitor, who will have to allow energy and time to go to the "Isle of Penelope," linked to the land by the slim isthmus of Corinth. We owe to the obstinate Schliemann the certainty that Mycenae and Tiryns were more than the inspired hallucinations of Homer's genius. The "gold town" can be reached through the Lion Gate. Archaeologists and art experts, architects and technicians had a field day here, equipped with goniometers and spirit-levels to measure, verify, and ascertain, by infinitesimal calculations, the engineering value of the monument. The citadel, 990 feet above sea level and surrounded by precipices, protected the treasure of Atreus, which is now at the National Archaeological Museum of Athens.

The powerful walls that surround nearby Tiryns provided the poetic backdrop for the labors of Hercules. The blocks of stone, which weigh from ten to thirteen tons and are twenty seven feet thick, continue to form a cyclopean defensive barrier. There is no more suitable description than "cyclopean," for, according to mythology, the building of the walls must be attributed to these powerful, one-eyed giants, pride of the Argos region. The amazed Pausanias stopped in Tiryns during his travels through ancient Greece on his way to the sanctuary at Epidaurus, and he commented that "Inside the enclosure neither human beings can die nor women can give birth; exactly the same rule is in force in Delos." In fact, just as they did in Delos, the holy island dedicated to Apollo, visitors had to take care not to disregard the imposed order and incur the gods' anger. Epidaurus was devoted to the cult of Asclepius, which claimed a cure for every disease and even the ability to revive the dead. The diagnosis would be communicated to the patient while he was asleep, when the god appeared to perform the miracle cure.

In Greece, theater had a religious significance; so Epidaurus too boasts an elegant marble semicircle that shines brightly through the opaque green of the pines and cypresses. Pausanias praised it: "Inside the Epidaurus Sanctuary there is a theater which, in my opinion, deserves to be visited more than any other; in fact, for splendor, the Roman theaters are superior to those in any other place, while, for size, the theater of Megalopolis in Arcadia excels. But what architect could compete with Polyclitus for harmony and beauty? Polyclitus is the architect of this theater and the circular building." Another source attributes this refined architecture to Polyclitus the younger, who lived a century later. The white limestone theater dates back to the fifth century B.C. and in the mid- to late

summer, still welcomes an audience enthusiastic for the old dramas, performed during the Epidaurus Festival.

Aristotle, in the *Metaphysics*, asserted: "All men aim to acknowledge nature," and nearby Laconia cannot be ignored by those who want to dedicate their holidays to this pastime. The lessons of history echo through the scattered fortresses that witnessed the Venetian rule and in the turreted houses in the small villages on the peninsula that stretches to the sea as far as Cape Matapan. The originality and the apparent precariousness of some of the human settlements is astonishing. Along the coast, the tiny island of Monemvasía will offer hospitality to those who are able to find it. The medieval village, crossed by narrow streets made for

The inventors of harmony

In 700 B.C., Greek architecture begins its developmental course, destined to make the wonderful landscape from the Peloponnesus to the Epirus and from Thrace to Attica an unequalled spectacle. The archaic period saw temples with sloping roofs resting on Doric and Ionic columns. Examples of this first period are Apollo's temple in Corinth, the Heraion in Argos, and the Brauron sanctuary. In the Classical Age, the works of genius and harmony are concentrated over a period of 150 years. Callicrates and Ictinus were the architects who embellished Athens by building the Parthenon and created schools in Delphi and Olympia, in Megalopolis and Messenia. In Delos and Pella, situated in Macedonia, are the most important masterly Corinthian works, a style introduced by Alexander the Great in the Hellenistic period. Finally, during the Roman Age, the Emperors Hadrian, Augustus, and Caesar had constructions built in Athens, Philippi, and Corinth, interpreting the Greek structural rules, materials, and shapes more imaginatively.

30 top *Phaistos Palace in Crete is one of the largest archaeological sites from the Minoan period. It is thirty-seven miles from Iraklion and is attributed to Rhadamanthys.*

30 bottom *Dodona theater, dating back to the third century B.C., came to light again in 1959. It has a diameter of 370 feet and could seat 15,000 spectators.*

31 *On Naxos Island, in the Cyclades, one can admire the imposing gateway to Apollo's Temple. It is the only trace of the archaic building which, undertaken in 340 A.D., was left unfinished.*

Delphi, the *omphalos* of the world

32-33 These two views of the Temple of Apollo reveal the intriguing spell of Delphi.

During the last century, the tiny village of Castri stood on the slopes of Mount Parnassus, isolated among the olive trees and wild bushes and sheltered by reddish rocks that became inflamed at sunset. In 1892, French archaeologists started excavations there to recover Apollo's Temple. Castri, since then completely lost, was rebuilt one kilometer west of the sheltered site, and it became more and more famous. The two rocky capes converging at the gorge where Castalian Spring gushes forth are called Phlembaukos and Rhodini ("burning" and "rose") and even (together) Phaedriades, or "shining." In ancient times, this landscape inspired the consecration of the place to the cult of Gaea, mother earth. In Greece, every site boasts its own mythological heritage.

34-35 *Athena's Temple is an imposing building surrounded by the sacred enclosure at Delphi. From the seventh to the sixth century B.C., the sanctuary was world renowned and became a center of diplomacy and a national symbol.*

Olympia, gymnasium of the gods

The shafts and capitals of columns are scattered in an apparent chaos, sharing light and shade. A visit to the ruins in the sacred enclosure of Olympia allows one to imagine the original framework of the palestra and the gymnasium in Hera's Temple, as well as the one in Zeus' Temple, housing the chryselephantine, or gold and ivory, statue by Phidias — one of the seven wonders of the ancient world — and even to daydream about treasures and riches offered by countries and sovereigns in the past. Here the Greeks came from far and wide in order to watch or take part in the Olympic games. The Spondophores, or sacred heralds, went through the country proclaiming *Ekecheiria*, the cease-fire that allowed the games to be conducted in peace. The competition included foot races, discus and javelin throwing, wrestling, boxing, cart races, and horse shows. In Olympia, the large stadium and the several buildings for athletes' training were situated in a luxuriant landscape. The *Kotinos*, the precious olive wreath worn by the winners, came from Altis, a wonderful forest whose olive trees were considered sacred.

The giants
of Peloponnesus

39 top *To enter Mycenae, a citadel, you have to pass through the Lion Gate which is sheltered with ramparts on both sides. This feline symbol, used in Cretan seals and throughout the Mycenaean culture, is monumental in the relief adorning the mighty arch.*

39 bottom *Corinth Hill keeps a precious example of Doric architecture in Apollo's Temple. Monolithic columns, severe and imposing, date back to 540 B.C. They are monumental in size and are visible from afar.*

In the labyrinth of the Minoan past

Crete, the largest Greek island, has some unique natural, ethnic, and historical attractions. The heterogeneous landscape is gifted with a mountainous structure varied with alternating caverns and cliffs, gorges and caves. The plain is fertile and cozy, the climate sweet and Mediterranean. Since 2,600 B.C., many ethnic groups have enjoyed these favorable conditions of life. People from Asia Minor landed on

the island, integrating with the Neolithic natives, who had come from Africa. The first European civilization was born here during the Minoic Bronze Age; it was a universe unto itself, with a complex religion different from the Greek one and supported by a firm, centralized economy. Moreover, the cheerful court society was extremely refined. The wonderful Palace of Knossos (shown here), discovered by Sir Arthur Evans in 1900, is representative of the taste of the time, with its original architecture and multicolored frescos. In the same way, the palaces in Mallia, Phaistos, A´yia Triáas, and Zakros, together with the opulent residences in Amnissos, Niru Chani, and Gournia, as well, acquaint the visitor with the myth and the reality of an ancient civilization, long forgotten.

41

The barren Delos,
cradle of Apollo

Myth tells us that on Delos, Leto gave birth to Apollo and the goddess Artemis. Moreover, this tiny island was said to be floating before Zeus anchored it to the seabed with granite columns. In ancient times, Delos had a very important religious role and was a destination for numerous pilgrimages. From 1000 B.C. to the Roman Age, the building of prestigious monuments was continuous. Traveling along Procession Road you can reach the Propylaea, which leads into Apollo's sanctuary. His cult began in about the eighth century. Here you can see the ruins of three temples dedicated to him and another to his sister Artemis, as well as Dionysus' sanctuary. Careful mosaics adorned the houses of the Tritons and Dionysus. From Mount Cynthus, 366 feet high, you can enjoy the view of the ruins.

42 *The famous Terrace of the Lions is situated along Procession Road. It boasts the most ancient Greek sculptures of animals, carved out of marble. The elegant felines date back to the seventh century B.C.; they face Sacred Lake, which was drained in 1925 in order to fight against malaria.*

43 *The ruins of Posidonias' house are still present as a reminder of the place where traders from ancient Beirut came to haggle and sell.*

44-45 *Delos Theater, dating back to the third century B.C., could seat up to 5,000 spectators.*

43

The islands
of early civilization

The inhabitants of the Greek islands succeeded in bringing out the beauty and harmony of the wonderful landscapes of their country. Architecture itself developed through original rules respecting nature. Technical devices were created in order to adapt the seats of a theater to the cavity of a valley; the Greeks appreciated their heterogeneous territory and were able to reach a formal purity, which they kept undamaged. Travelers and tourists can see, today as in ancient times, the spectacular stalactites and stalagmites in the Cyclops cavern in Ghioura, a tiny island near Cape Skinari, on Zante. Also on Zante, one can venture by boat out to the caverns, which have inspired so many fishermen's legends, hollowed out in the cliff. Tours of the region are as popular as ever, and every year they offer a glimpse of the migratory behavior of the thousands of butterflies that, from June to September, meet in Petaloudes Valley in Rhodes, painting the sky thousands of colors.

46 top *The island of Mykonos, offering glimpses of white terraces and small balconies, stretches out into the Aegean Sea. Within the labyrinth of lanes are an interesting archaeological museum and a picturesque folklore museum.*

46 below *The small port on the island of Sími is situated eighteen miles from Rhodes. Here, shops and inns are housed in neoclassical buildings arranged as an amphitheater, a remnant of the Roman rule.*

47 *Near Lindos, the coasts of Rhodes have rough, jagged rock walls.*

Zante, flower of the East

The blue of the sea that fills the gulfs and inlets frames the cliffs of Zante, the most southern of the Ionian Islands. This sea seems to invite the legend telling of the goddess Venus's birth from these waters, as Botticelli depicted. On Lagana Beach, other creatures surface from the sea; at predictable times a particular species of turtle arrives to lay their eggs; for years, these turtles have kept a regular appointment with the great cycle of life on these beaches.

50-51 *A cliff along the steep western coast slopes down to the sea in Zante, the island celebrated by Italian Romantic poet Ugo Foscolo in his famous verse.*

Corfu, the enchanted island

52-53 *These two photographs show different views of Kanoni on the island of Corfu. The whitewashed building is the monastery of Vlacherna. Behind it you can see Pondikonisi, the "island of the mice." According to legend, the island was once a ship of the Phaeacians, who took Odysseus to Ithaca. The ship was turned to stone by Poseidon.*

54-55 *In a small port on Corfu, the multicolored ships wait to sail toward the open sea.*

56 top *North of Corfu, near Korakana, a luxuriant vegetation composed of olive trees and cypresses covers the hillsides.*

56 bottom *Inland, on Corfu, hidden by a thick wood, small houses are secluded.*

57 *Paleokastritsa beach may be the site where an exhausted Odysseus came ashore, welcomed by the young Nausicaa, daughter of Alcinous, king of the Phaeacians, ancient natives of Corfu.*

58-59 *Cephalonia, the largest of the Ionian islands, affords another glimpse of paradise.*

The capricious breezes of the *meltemi*

The tiny island of Mykonos is considered the truly Greek island by the Athenians, who choose it for their holidays. Coffee bars and pubs, numerous nightclubs and restaurants make it famous all over the world. In the chief town of the island, the small cube-shaped houses are fitted above one another, making a terrace out of each roof. Every year, the impeccable white walls are painted, but only the churches — which number 365, one for every day of the year — boast blue domes that disappear against the sky. The religious buildings, many of them erected through the generosity of private citizens, differ in shape and size. The most famous is Paraportiani, whose ground floor was built on the same site where four small chapels once stood in succession.

62-63 In Mykonos, from the Hill of Mills you can see the busy and colorful port. When the meltemi *blows, reaching the island can be a difficult exercise.*

White geometry in the sun

In the Cyclades, the architecture dates back to 1700. The tendency of residential complexes to be fortified up to the highest spur had a defensive purpose; in fact, in 1500 and 1600, raids by Turkish pirates were very common. The laid bricks of the houses, of stone or slate, were left in their natural state in order to deceive the enemy coming from the sea; the typical plaster was introduced later, in times of peace.

Thera, the beautiful island where the myth of Atlantis survives

Through time, many people have subscribed to the theory that the island of Thera is a fragment of the legendary Atlantis. Was this utopian island, so dear to Plato, destroyed by a mighty eruption in ancient times? The crescent-moon-shaped cliff that drops to the Aegean sea, its rocks inflamed at sunset, seems to support this idea for the more romantic at heart.

Shining bays and dark blue inlets

The Sporades are a group of scattered islands situated in the Aegean Sea and making up the most eastern Greek archipelago. The most northern and scattered group is linked to the Magnesia peninsula, while the southern islands follow one another until they reach Rhodes. From an historical and artistic point of view, these islands could not boast a leading role in the past, but now they have become frequent destinations for tourists and consequently play an important role in the economy of the country.

72 top *The small chief town of the island of Skiathos stands out on a bay along the southwestern coast, where inlets gladden the picturesque marine landscape. This small town shares the same history as the continent, which is only three miles away.*

72 bottom and 73 *The chief town on the island of Skopelos dominates a bay turned towards the north, its slopes covered with cultivated terraces. In these photographs, stone tiles arranged in a circular pattern on the dome of a church have been whitewashed; the town's inhabitants imaginatively employ bricks and tiles to decorate the roofs of houses and churches; of the latter, there are about a hundred and twenty.*

Aegina "the rich"

History was generous with the island of Aegina. Findings dating back to the fourth century B.C. indicate that the island has been inhabited since that period. It fought a long time against Athens for naval supremacy, and in 456 B.C., it defeated the powerful Egyptian fleet. In 480 B.C., on the highest peak of the island, the renowned temple of Afaia was built and is still considered one of the most important temples of the past. In order to preserve the numerous memories of this island and to understand their value, a small museum has been built and traces the island's history from the Neolithic to the Roman period.

Sloped terraces along Gaea's side

76 *Epicurus, Pythagoras, and Polycrates were born on the island of Samos, in the northeast Aegean Sea.*

77 top *According to Homer, Poseidon could see the battles of Troy from the island of Samothrace.*

77 bottom *On the island of Thaxos, rural houses blend with a fertile landscape.*

Rhodes, the island fortress

The checkered map of the city of Rhodes was planned in 408 B.C. by the architect Hippodamus. After visiting the city, geographer Strabo said: "Port, streets, walls, and buildings are much superior to those in any other town; we do not know better or even similar examples of it." Rhodes is divided into the "New Town," the "Old Medieval Town" (the only intact example of one in the country) surrounded by the fortified walls built by the knights of St. John, and the "Old Town," with the Acropolis. Rhodes is the symbol of the whole island and carries the marks of a magnificent history.

78 In ancient times, in the picturesque port of Mandrakhi, the Colossus of Rhodes welcomed the sailors. One of the seven wonders of the ancient world, it was destroyed by an earthquake in 227 B.C. The Greek sculptor Chares worked for twelve years on the huge bronze statue.

79 top In Knights' Hospital, built between 1440 and 1489, findings dating back to the Mycenaean and Roman periods can be admired in the collection of the Archaeological Museum.

79 bottom *From the Marine Gate it is possible to enter the Old Town, which offers a large collection of Byzantine, Latin, and Turkish architecture.*

80-81 *The powerful fortifications of the Old Town in Rhodes, seen here from the port, contain the principal monuments of the island. A complex network of winding lanes crossed by arches leads to large squares shaded by plane trees.*

82-83 *The Acropolis preserves the remains of three temples — those of Zeus and Athena, which date back to the third century, and that of Apollo. Moreover, there is a recently restored stadium and quadrangular theater where, in summer, the classic tragedies are performed.*

Myths and legends in the Islands

84-85 *A few miles from the western coast of Rhodes is the small rectangular island of Khalki. The square houses are like a painted scene — a cubist fantasy for the sailors who come to dock in this seldom frequented part of the country.*

86 *A deep inlet interrupts the coastline on the island of Kalimnos, an island in the Dodecanese, well known for natural sponges.*

87 *Astipalaia belongs geographically to the Cyclades, but historically it has many more relationships with the Dodecanese. History has been generous with this island; a stately fortress from the Venetian domination stands out from the highest rock of the island, while along the bare slope, residential areas have been developed.*

88-89 These two images depict the citadel in Cora on the island of Patmos. The small, quiet community characterized by a complex urbanization consists of monasteries, churches, and chapels devoted to the cult of St. John. Tradition says that it was here the Saint wrote the Apocalypse, the prophetic text, in a cave in the first century A.D.

90-91 The chief harbor on the island of Simi, very near Rhodes, is situated in a quiet bay on the northern coast. The houses of the small town are arranged as in a crescent along the mountainous slope.

92-93 This may look like a "genre painting" made by a careful landscape painter of the last century; on the contrary, this image represents modern, everyday life on the island of Karpathos.

The land of milk and honey

Crete, the largest island in the Greek archipelago, almost equidistant from Peloponnesus, the Cyclades, Rhodes, and Libya, was a cultural and artistic crossroads. The palaces in Knossos, Mallia, Phaistos, A´yia Triás, and Zakros are from the Myceanean period. In Gortyna and Lato, the magnificence of ancient Greece under Roman rule is evoked; Panagia Kirà, near Krista, as well as in the church of Hagios Titos, are solemn and stately monuments of the Byzantine style. In Candia, fortresses, yards, and fountains are the harmonious inheritance of the Venetian domination. Mosques reveal the decorative style of the Turkish tradition.

94 *Iraklion, once called Candia, was converted by the Venetians into a fortified citadel with the aim of withstanding the Turkish siege.*

95 *The shores of Crete offer images of incomparable beauty.*

96-97 *Visitors can enjoy meals by candlelight in the typical seaside restaurants in Rethimnon, on the coast between Iraklion and Candia.*

The city contested by the gods

History tells about people — for example, the inhabitants of Athens, Sparta, Thebes, and Aegina — now meditative, now warlike, who fought for the possession of the land and the sea, according to the desires of leaders and strategists. Today, democracy has been reestablished and the unity of the country has been rebuilt.
The political center of the country is its capital. At the beginning of the 19th century, Athens looked like a neglected and inefficient small town. The modern capital dates back to the reign of Otto I (1834-1862); the plan to transform public buildings and maps of the town was made by a group of architects whose nationalities were heterogeneous; there were two Germans, two Danes, one Frenchman, and one Greek.

98 top *A colorful picture of the small port where the yachts dock on arrival in Athens.*

98 bottom *The modern Olympic stadium was built in the same location as the ancient stadium in which Olympic games took place.*

99 *Dionysus Theater was built in a natural setting. Here, the first glorious works of the three great Attic playwrights — Sophocles, Euripides, and Aeschylus — were performed.*

The arch of Hadrian, the Stadium, the Olympion, and the Ceramicus — Athens is huge, but the classical marble structures that represent the ancient vestiges of the past are so numerous that one can easily trace an amazing and rich archaeological history here. Each Athenian would probably suggest a different place, according to his own personality.

The most serious inhabitant would direct your attention to the street where the University is situated. Here, three neoclassical buildings, built in the last century, follow one another — the National Library, the University, and the Academy. The admirers of the social and political ideals of their ancestors would suggest you take the route that leads

Agorà, where the destiny of the *polis* was decided daily. Moreover, they would lead you to the Metroum (the official archives), the Bouleuterion (the senate), and the Tholos (where fifty senators lived at the state's expense). Everyone would recommend a visit to the Acropolis (on the left in the photograph); the pride of Athens, it always meets or surpasses visitors' expectations. The steep, calcareous cliff that dominates the capital has been the destination of both conquerors and travelers for 3,000 years. The building of the most harmonious architectural complex of ancient times we owe to Pericles, the renowned Athenian. He financed, beginning in 454 B.C., sculptures and structures of white "pentelikon" (painted in red, blue, and gold tones, according to the custom of the time) in order to rebuild the town previously destroyed by the Persian conquest.

102-103 The Parthenon was decorated by 92 metopes representing mythological battles, 44 statues placed in the pediments, and 525 feet of engraved friezes that portrayed the procession of the Panathenaea.

The name Parthenon means "Room of the Virgin." Originally, the name referred to a room of the temple dedicated to Athena, but then it was given to the entire building. The Parthenon was built on previously existing foundations between 447 and 432 B.C., and since that time it has suffered several misfortunes. In 1460, it was even turned into a mosque, and later, in 1687, a minaret was added that was later destroyed. Still later, twenty-eight columns were destroyed when the artillery of the Venetian fleet hit the gunpowder the Turks had unwisely stored there.

The capital of the recovered democracy

The city of Athens spreads out between two hills — Mount Lycabettus and the Acropolis. It incorporates both and reaches towards Piraeus and the sea. The lively center develops between two poles: Syntagma Square, which is overlooked by the ancient Royal Palace, is now the seat of Parliament, and Omonoia Square is the hub from which three large streets branch out.

The heroes of independence

In Syntagma Square, the Parliament stands opposite the Monument to the Unknown Warrior. In front of the latter, the ritual (common to most European capitals) of the changing of the guard takes place. The traditional uniforms of the *euzoni*, the Greek soldiers, are unique and consist of a sheer tunic, a white leotard, a richly embroidered waistcoat, a red fez, and unusual shoes with "bent" toes.

From land to sea, the tastes of the Mediterranean

Codfish, mullet, tuna, and sole, crawfish, mussels, squid, and large, tasty octopus enrich the Mediterranean cuisine in restaurants and picturesque country taverns from Macedonia to Peloponnesus and from the Ionian Islands to the Sporades. But the huge quantity of fish and seafood products cramming the stalls of the covered market in Athens is deceptive; in fact, within the economy of the country, fishing is not very profitable, because continuous exploitation has depleted the marine population and compelled the inhabitants of the islands, most of them fishermen, to import these products. Agriculture is very different; in fact, Greek commerce is based on agriculture. Olives, wine, and honey have been, since ancient times, the main features of a gastronomic culture that enjoys a strong Turkish influence.

The monasteries: austerity and community

Greece has always enjoyed a privileged relationship with things metaphysical. Universal thoughts absorb the continent and the island and form an important part of the national identity. Saints and blessed souls crowd the orthodox calendar, increasing the occasions to celebrate. Corfu deserves a visit on the holiday of St. Spiridione, while the day of the Virgin is celebrated in Paros with the eating of fish and the drinking of wine, and in Siatista by equestrian games. In Greece, it is often possible to see long processions during the celebration of the saint of a town or on Christmas night, when every village, both island and continental, resonates with the chorus of the people singing the "Kalanda."

114 *Zographou and Dochiarion monasteries are situated on the southwest coast of Athos peninsula. Zographou, shown in the top picture, follows the cenobitic rule, according to which life must be led in complete community. On the contrary, Dochiarion, in the bottom picture, is faithful to the idiorrhythmic rule that, aside from common prayers, allows for personal asceticism.*

115 *During the celebration of the patron saint, the believers carry an ancient icon of the Virgin Mary in a procession originating from Iviron monastery on Mount Athos.*

In the sky, to elevate the spirit

Popular belief attributes these huge rocky columns that seem to separate the sky from the land to meteors. On the contrary, the sea, which once covered the plain, shaped these surreal "sculptures." In the 14th century, through monasteries, man colonized these twenty-four strong spires that look as if they are

suspended in the sky. In the past, ascetics and visitors were lifted and lowered in a basket supported by a rope. Today, the original winches are still employed, but in the 1920s, tunnels were excavated in the rock as an alternative means of reaching the surface.

116 *This panoramic view of Thessaly is suggestive of the original theory of a landscape carved by meteors.*

117 *Varlaam monastery, built in 1517, houses a museum and a library.*

Eastern shapes for the domes of Mistras

In Laconia, four miles from Sparta, the small town of Mistras stands dominated by a hill where a citadel was built. From the 13th to the 15th centuries, it was the residence of the Byzantine princes, whose courts were the centers of literary and philosophic studies. These late Byzantine buildings went to ruin after the Turkish domination

and have been restored only in this century. Notable among them is the Perivleptos monastery, built in the second half of the 14th century. Inside, the walls and the vaults of the rooms are richly frescoed with precious paintings in the Byzantine style.

The "republic" suspended in silence

According to the belief of the local monks, the Virgin Mary, while traveling to Cyprus to meet Lazarus, was carried by the winds to Mount Athos, causing the pagan idols worshipped by the natives to crumble. The Virgin Mary, pleased with this event, declared the mount to be her own private garden, forbidden to any other woman. In 1060, Emperor Constantine IX issued an edict through which "every woman, female animal, child, eunuch, or any person with clean-shaven face" would be barred from the mount. Today, cruise ships, since they carry women passengers, must stop 500 meters from the shore inhabited by the bearded followers of Athanasius, the founding saint, who established both the monastic rule and the convent plan. Each monastery has a quadrangular shape and is made up of many wood and stone floors. In the center of the courtyard that holds churches and chapels is the Katholikon, the church where the community gathers for religious services. Some believers still live in the hermitages scattered over 200 square miles of luxuriant vegetation, while others live in small communities called Skites. The republic has suffered an inevitable decay, because today few novices are interested in the monastic life.

120 top *Dochiariou monastery on the west coast follows the idiorrhythmic system, where the monk has the opportunity to manage his spiritual life according to his own "rhythm."*

120 bottom *Simonos Petra monastery is one of the twelve monasteries that follow the cenobic rule; the monks live together and share every activity.*

121 right *A monk leads the horses carrying food supplies to water.*

Since 1977, the lay members of the Orthodox Church have been authorized to visit the monastic republic in Athos and spend no more than four nights there for religious and scientific reasons. Any newcomer who is interested in this unusual

experience will have to produce a letter from the consulate of his nation to the Greek Ministry of Foreign Affairs. No more than ten authorizations per day are granted. This opportunity allows the visitor to penetrate the spirit of severe religious rule and to observe the various tasks the monks perform daily. In the past, each monk was assigned a particular task, but today, the lack of novices forces the monks to undertake varied activities.

Severe lines and gold iridescence

124-125 *These mural paintings represent the rhythmic cadence of the pantheon depicting the saints in Byzantine iconography. The images are from the church of the Iviron monastery.*

126-127 *The Great Lavra monastery, which follows the idiorrhythmic system, is situated on the northeastern coast of Mount Athos.*

Photo Credits:

Marcello Bertinetti/White Star archives: Pages 2-3; 4-5; 6-7; 16; 20; 21; 23; 25; 26; 27; 84-85; 98; 99; 100-101; 102-103; 104; 105; 106; 107; 108-109; 110; 111; 112; 113; 114; 115; 120; 121; 122; 123; 124; 125; 126-127.

Angela Bertinetti/White Star archives: Page 36 bottom.

Graziano Arici/Grazia Neri: Page 36 top.

F.R. Bergmann/Zefa: Page 94.

A. Boano/Panda Photo: Page 22.

R. Bouquet/Diaf: Page 60.

Elio Ciol/Grazia Neri: Page 40.

Anne Conway: Pages 28-29; 47; 53; 54-55; 56; 57; 77 bottom; 78; 79; 86; 88; 89; 90-91.

Guido Cozzi/SIE: Pages 92-93.

Dallas & John Eaton/Apa Photo Agency: Pages 32; 34-35; 38; 46 top; 62-63; 116; 117; Back-Cover

Damm/Zefa: Pages 8; 42; 44-45; 80-81; 82-83.

J. P. Durand/Diaf: Page 74.

Eich/Zefa: Page 46 bottom.

A. Eteve/Diaf: Page 68.

Michael Friedel/Grazia Neri: Page 65 bottom.

Jean Gabanou/Diaf: Pages 9; 65 top; 72; 128.

Robert Harding: Pages 1; 17; 58-59; 70-71; 75; 76.

Konrad Helbig/Zefa: Pages 30 top; 37; 119.

Hoffman/Zefa: Page 87.

Simeone Huber/SIE: Cover, pages 12-13; 31; 48; 49; 50-51; 73.

K. Kerth/Zefa: Pages 39 bottom; 118.

Ludwig/Zefa: Page 39 top.

Luetticke/Zefa: Page 95.

Rassias/Diaf: Pages 24; 77 top.

G. Saltini/Panda Photo: Page 69.

Michael Short/Robert Harding: Pages 18-19.

Ben Simmons/Diaf: Page 61.

Starfoto/Zefa: Page 30 bottom.

Daniel Thierry/Diaf: Pages 33; 52.

Sandro Vannini/Panda Photo: Pages 14-15.

World Pictures: Pages 43; 96-97.

Zefa: Pages 10-11; 41; 64; 66-67.